Card in Back →

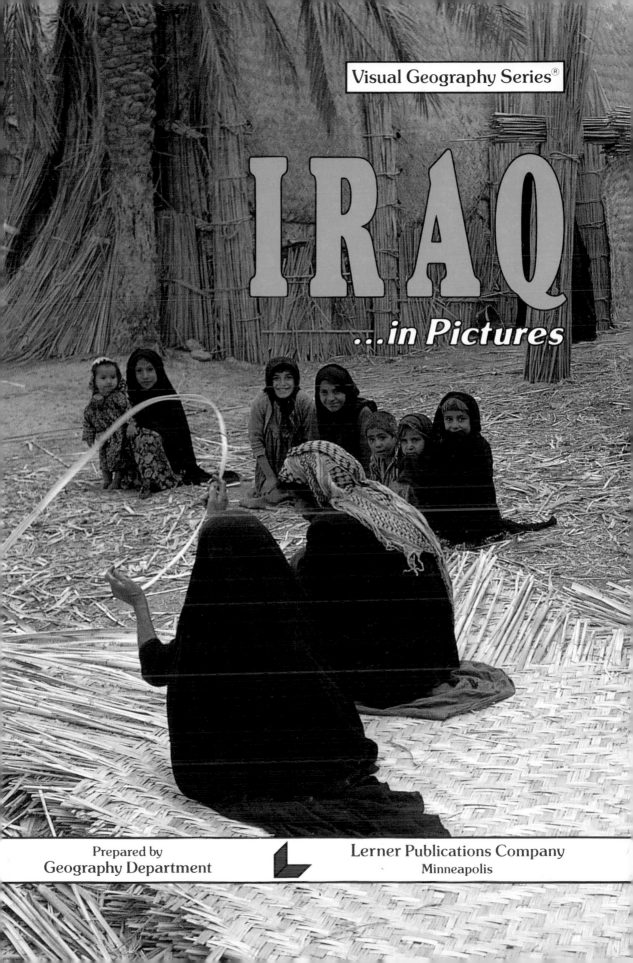

Visual Geography Series®

# IRAQ
## ...in Pictures

Prepared by
**Geography Department**

**Lerner Publications Company**
Minneapolis

956.7
I
c.1

Photo by EDR Media

**National vaccination programs help to protect Iraqi children from childhood diseases.**

This book is an all-new edition in the Visual Geography Series. Previous editions were published by Sterling Publishing Company, New York City. The text, set in 10/12 Century Textbook, is fully revised and updated, and new photographs, maps, charts, and captions have been added.

LIBRARY OF CONGRESS CATALOGING-IN-PUBLICATION DATA

Iraq in pictures.

(Visual geography series)
Rev. ed. of: Iraq in pictures / prepared by Jon A. Teta.
Includes index.
Summary: Photographs and text introduce the geography, history, government, people, and economy of Iraq, the cradle of civilization.
1. Iraq. [1. Iraq] I. Teta, John A. Iraq in pictures. II. Lerner Publications Company. Geography Dept. III. Series: Visual geography series (Minneapolis, Minn.)
DS70.6.I735    1990         956.7         89–8351
ISBN 0-8225-1847-3

International Standard Book Number: 0-8225-1847-3
Library of Congress Catalog Card Number: 89-8351

## VISUAL GEOGRAPHY SERIES®

**Publisher**
Harry Jonas Lerner
**Associate Publisher**
Nancy M. Campbell
**Senior Editor**
Mary M. Rodgers
**Editors**
Gretchen Bratvold
Dan Filbin
**Photo Researcher**
Karen A. Sirvaitis
**Editorial/Photo Assistant**
Marybeth Campbell
**Consultants/Contributors**
Isaac Eshel
Dr. Ruth F. Hale
Sandra K. Davis
**Designer**
Jim Simondet
**Cartographer**
Carol F. Barrett
**Indexers**
Kristine S. Schubert
Sylvia Timian
**Production Manager**
Gary J. Hansen

Photo by EDR Media

**Dressed in traditional Islamic clothing, Iraqi women carry baskets to the local mosque (place of prayer).**

## Acknowledgments

Title page photo by EDR Media.

Elevation contours adapted from *The Times Atlas of the World*, seventh comprehensive edition (New York: Times Books, 1985).

3  4  5  6  7  8  9  10  99  98  97  96  95  94  93  92  91

Workers in Baghdad, the capital of Iraq, arrange freshly formed bricks to dry in the sun.

# Contents

TURKEY

SYRIA

IRAN

JORDAN

SAUDI ARABIA

KUWAIT

PERSIAN GULF

Tall Afar
NINEVEH RUINS
Mosul
NIMRUD RUINS (CALAH)
Erbil
Kirkuk
Samarra
Tharthar Res.
Kadhimain
Lake Habbaniya
BAGHDAD
CTESIPHON RUINS
Bahr al-Milh
Karbala
BABYLON RUINS
Al Kufa
Al-Najaf
Kadisiya
Lake Sadiya
Amara
Al-Nasiriya
Al-Qurna
L. Hammar
Basra
Abadan
Zubayr
Rumayla
Umm Qasr
Fao
IRAQI-SAUDI ARABIAN NEUTRAL ZONE

Pipeline
Great Zab R.
Little Zab R.
Wadi
Adhaim R.
Diyala R.
Euphrates
Tigris R.
Pipeline
Wadi
Wadi
Wadi
Wadi
Shatt al-Arab
Pipeline

## IRAQ

N
↑

- - - - Governorate Boundaries

———— Major Roads

| 0 | 50 | 100 Miles |
| 0 | 50 | 100 Kilometers |

MIDDLE EAST
IRAQ

INDIAN OCEAN

| 0 | 500 Miles |
| 0 | 500 Kilometers |

20°
20°
40°
60°

## METRIC CONVERSION CHART
### To Find Approximate Equivalents

| WHEN YOU KNOW: | MULTIPLY BY: | TO FIND: |
|---|---|---|
| **AREA** | | |
| acres | 0.41 | hectares |
| square miles | 2.59 | square kilometers |
| **CAPACITY** | | |
| gallons | 3.79 | liters |
| **LENGTH** | | |
| feet | 30.48 | centimeters |
| yards | 0.91 | meters |
| miles | 1.61 | kilometers |
| **MASS (weight)** | | |
| pounds | 0.45 | kilograms |
| tons | 0.91 | metric tons |
| **VOLUME** | | |
| cubic yards | 0.77 | cubic meters |
| **TEMPERATURE** | | |
| degrees Fahrenheit | 0.56 (*after* subtracting 32) | degrees Celsius |

Vendors at a stall in a Baghdad bazaar (open-air market) offer customers a colorful variety of goods from many countries, as well as fruits and grains from Iraq.

# Introduction

Located in southwestern Asia, the Republic of Iraq is a major power in the Middle East. Various peoples have inhabited the country for thousands of years, and the ruins of many ancient cities lie within the nation's boundaries.

Sumerian, Babylonian, Assyrian, and Chaldean cultures once flourished in Iraq. They have left behind evidence of great ac-

complishments in trade, science, agriculture, and literature. Iraq came under the control of an Arab empire in the seventh century. The conquering Arabs introduced the Islamic religion, which has become a cornerstone of the nation's identity. Members of Islam's two main sects—the Sunnis and the Shiites—live in Iraq. In addition to Arab peoples, the country contains Islamic minorities, such as the Kurds. They make up the largest non-Arab segment of the population.

Until the 1920s, the region's wealth and fame came from the Tigris and Euphrates rivers. Between these two parallel waterways lies some of the world's most fertile soil. But for centuries the land's agricultural productivity varied according to how well people controlled the flooding of the rivers. When farmers were able to manage

Made of hard stone, this carved statue depicts Gudea, who governed the Sumerian city-state of Lagash from about 2144 to 2124 B.C. The few records of his rule that exist portray Gudea as a just, cultured, and peace-loving leader.

Children, parents, and elderly people crowd the archway of a mosque in Baghdad. The Islamic religion has been an important part of Iraqi society since the seventh century A.D., when Islamic armies conquered the area.

the floodwaters, the region prospered. On the other hand, invaders weakened local resistance by smashing the canals and ruining the land.

Since the early twentieth century, when Iraq came under British rule, the country's wealth has depended on a different source —oil. Vast amounts of this vital fuel lie within Iraq. When Iraq gained independence in 1932, it allowed foreign investors to develop its oil resources. In 1972 the Iraqi government took over the extraction, processing, and export of the nation's petroleum.

Between 1980 and 1988, a costly war with neighboring Iran kept Iraq from earning a large income from oil. Bombing raids destroyed petroleum facilities in both countries, and casualties numbered in the hundreds of thousands. The United Nations arranged a cease-fire between the two countries in August 1988, and each side began to rebuild its economy.

Internal tensions continue, however. A hostile relationship exists between the government and the Kurdish population. Iraqi Kurds fought on the side of Iran during the war. The Iraqi government has taken harsh measures—reportedly including the use of lethal poison gas—to subdue the Kurds.

In some ways, Iraq emerged from the war a stronger country. Its socialist government remains firmly in charge of national affairs, and Iraq has the support of many other Arab states in the region. Yet the nation's responses to its greatest problems—Kurdish unrest, a large war debt, and postwar relations with Iran—will determine how unified and secure Iraq will be in the future.

Independent Picture Service

Throughout the 1980s, Iraq's petroleum facilities—such as this complex in Basra—were subject to Iranian bombings. The war between Iran and Iraq weakened the ability of both sides to export oil—each country's main source of foreign income.

7

Much of Iraq's soil can support farming. Local workers use long-handled tools to tend the fields, which must be carefully irrigated to produce crops.

Photo by EDR Media

# 1) The Land

Located at the northern end of the Persian Gulf, the Republic of Iraq covers an area of about 168,000 square miles. The nation is slightly larger than the state of California. Turkey and Syria border Iraq to the north and northwest, and Jordan lies to the west. Iran is Iraq's eastern neighbor, and Kuwait and Saudi Arabia are located to the south. The southeastern corner of Iraq touches the Persian Gulf.

## Topography

Iraq has three main topographical regions. A wide, flat plain lies in the center of the country. Deserts are located in the west and southwest, and mountains separate the northeastern part of Iraq from Iran.

The plain is divided into upper and lower sections. The Upper Plain begins north of the city of Samarra between the Tigris and Euphrates rivers and extends into Turkey and Syria. Highlands in the region reach heights of 1,000 feet above sea level, and rolling grasslands are common. Deep valleys cut through the Upper Plain, leaving higher areas dry and hard to irrigate.

The Lower Plain reaches south from Samarra to the Persian Gulf. This part of the plain is alluvial—that is, it consists of a mixture of clay, sand, rocks, and silt that have been deposited through centuries of flooding. The Lower Plain includes a delta, or fertile area, at the mouths of the Tigris and Euphrates. Most of the country's population live in this region. Just south of the delta—near the city of Al-Qurna—the land becomes marshy. The Madan, or Marsh Arabs, inhabit the swampland, living in arched dwellings built of reeds.

A section of the Syrian Desert lies in western Iraq, and in the southwest is another desert, Al-Hajara, which extends into Saudi Arabia. The nation's hot zones —which are flat, rocky, and sparsely vegetated—contain several wadis (dry riverbeds). When seasonal rains come, these wadis can fill up, releasing short, devastating floods as the riverbeds swiftly channel water through the level landscape.

Iraq's portion of the Syrian Desert hosts few Bedouin nomadic Arab clans that

At the southern edge of Iraq, the land becomes marshy where the waters of the Tigris and Euphrates rivers meet. Some Iraqis build reed homes on the swampland and fish the local waters for food.

Photo by EDR Media

Photo by EDR Media

Herders guide their flocks through hot, dry areas of the country in search of water and scrub vegetation for their livestock.

inhabit the desert. Al-Hajara, on the other hand, is a frequent stop for desert nomads. At the southern edge of Al-Hajara is the diamond-shaped Iraqi–Saudi Arabian Neutral Zone. It was established in 1975 to ease the Bedouin's seasonal movements between the two countries.

In northeastern Iraq are the Zagros Mountains, which extend into Iran. The range has many peaks above 9,000 feet. The highest summits in Iraq are Haji Ibrahim (11,811 feet) and Siyah Kuh (11,739 feet). In the foothills and valleys of the Zagros Mountains live most of Iraq's Kurdish people, who form a strong, non-Arab minority of the population. The region also contains some of Iraq's richest oil fields.

## Rivers and Lakes

Iraq's two main rivers—the Tigris and the Euphrates—have carried fertile soil to nearby river valleys for centuries. The Tigris starts its 1,180-mile course in Turkey's Lake Van. The Euphrates rises

Independent Picture Service

Northeastern Iraq features jagged hills through which local streams cut narrow routes.

Independent Picture Service

During winter, deep snow covers the Zagros Mountains, which Iraq and Iran share.

10

Giant waterwheels dot the banks of the Euphrates River in both Syria and Iraq. The devices bring water from the river to nearby fields for irrigation.

in eastern Turkey and has a total length of 2,235 miles. At the point where the rivers flow into Iraq, 25 miles of open plain separate them from each other. The Tigris flows south, and the Euphrates takes a southeastern direction.

The Euphrates has no tributaries in Iraq. The Tigris, on the other hand, is fed by several waterways, including the Great Zab, Little Zab, Diyala, and Adhaim rivers. Many lakes also have formed in the Tigris-Euphrates Valley. Lake Habbaniya lies just west of the Euphrates. Lake Hammar and Lake Sadiya are in the southern part of the Lower Plain.

At Al-Qurna, the waters of the Tigris and the Euphrates combine to form the Shatt al-Arab. This 120-mile-long channel connects the port of Basra with the Persian Gulf. Oceangoing vessels reach Basra by way of this broad waterway.

Iraq and its eastern neighbor, Iran, have long vied for control of the strategic Shatt

Shaded by tall date palms, the Shatt al-Arab flows toward the Persian Gulf. This 120-mile channel forms part of the Iran-Iraq border and connects the Iraqi port of Basra with the gulf.

11

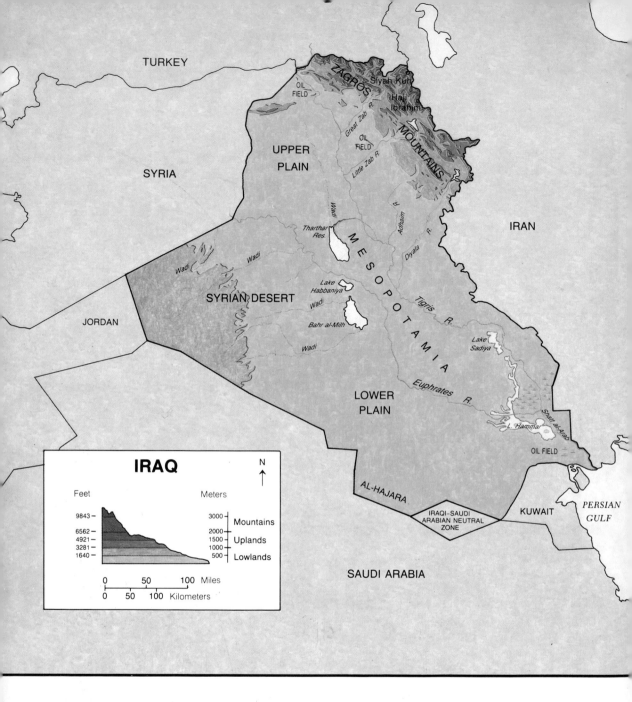

IRAQ

Feet          Meters
              N
              ↑

9843 —        3000 — Mountains
6562 —        2000 —
4921 —        1500 — Uplands
3281 —        1000 —
1640 —         500 — Lowlands

0      50     100 Miles
0    50  100  Kilometers

al-Arab. Part of the waterway flows between the two countries. The area was heavily bombed in the Iran-Iraq war of the 1980s. Iraq controls the entire channel, as well as the port of Fao, where the Shatt al-Arab enters the Persian Gulf. Abadan, Iran's oil-refining city, lies along the waterway's banks.

## Flora and Fauna

In the Zagros Mountains, overcutting and overgrazing have reduced some of Iraq's oak forests to scrubland. Stands of other trees—maple, hawthorn, and pistachio, for example—remain, however. At higher elevations are alpine plants that can survive harsh weather.

Reeds, boxthorns, buttercups, rushes, and saltbush grow in the nation's plains and marshlands. Date palms thrive in many parts of the country, and, occasionally, poplars and willows appear. Drought-resistant vegetation—such as rockrose, storksbill, and catchfly—cover desert areas. In the spring, when the rains come, these plants bloom and provide food for sheep, goats, and camels.

Centuries of human settlement have depleted Iraq's wildlife. Surviving mammals include bats, rats, jackals, hyenas, and wildcats, with wild pigs and gazelles living in remote areas. Reptiles are numerous, and lizards and snakes make their homes in the country's deserts. Among Iraq's domesticated animals are camels, oxen, water buffalo, and horses. Northern Iraqis raise large flocks of sheep and goats for their wool and skins.

Iraq's game birds include wild ducks, geese, black partridges, bustards, and sand grouse. Birds of prey—such as vultures, eagles, hawks, and buzzards—feed on small mammals. The Tigris, the Euphrates, and the Shatt al-Arab contain freshwater fish, which are an important part of the Iraqi diet.

## Climate

The plain of Iraq experiences hot, dry summers. The highest temperatures, which usually occur between June and September, exceed 100° F. Records show much hotter temperature readings—up to more than 120° F—in regions along the Persian Gulf. Average summer temperatures in the deserts reach the nineties. Mountain areas of Iraq are cool in summer, with sharp temperature drops at night.

Photo by EDR Media

Members of a Bedouin family tend their camels, which can survive in the hot, dry areas of southern and eastern Iraq.

Winters (December through March), although sometimes cold, are generally mild and sunny. On the plain, average winter figures hover around 40° F, and temperatures in the deserts drop to about 30° F. In the mountainous northeast, however, temperatures fall well below freezing.

Except in the Zagros Mountains, average annual rainfall ranges between four and eight inches. In the highest elevations of the northeast, yearly precipitation figures of 40 inches are not uncommon, and snow frequently falls on the highest peaks. The deserts receive little, if any, rainfall.

Iraq has two wind patterns. The eastern wind, called a *sharki*, is hot, dry, and dusty. Sharki winds blow from April to June and from September to November. Their strong gusts can reach 50 miles per hour and often kick up huge walls of dust. The other pattern, known as a *shamal*, is a steady, northern wind that brings relief from the extreme heat of summer.

## Natural Resources

Aside from its vast oil reserves, Iraq has few minerals. Recent geological surveys have shown, however, that usable deposits of sulfur, salt, coal, gypsum (used in making plaster), lead, and zinc exist.

One of the leading oil-producing countries of the world, Iraq contains large reserves of crude oil. Primary oil fields lie near Kirkuk between the Zagros Mountains and the Upper Plain, in the Zubayr-Rumayla region west of Basra, and in places near the city of Mosul.

## Baghdad

Located on both banks of the Tigris River, Baghdad—the capital of Iraq—is a teeming center of trade, manufacturing, and culture. The nation's largest city, Baghdad contains more than three million people, most of whom are Muslims (followers of the Islamic religion).

The heart of Baghdad is made up of two districts—a modern section on the west bank of the Tigris and an ancient one on the east bank. The old part of the city—with its narrow streets and noisy bazaars (open-air markets)—has been inhabited for centuries. In recent years, modern structures, including hotels and banks, have

Outside Kirkuk—northern Iraq's main oil-processing center—fires burn continuously from the natural gas that lies just beneath the ground.

14

An aerial view of Kadhimain shows visitors strolling in the courtyard of a mosque. Located on the Tigris River within the metropolitan area of Baghdad, the holy place is the burial site of two important leaders of the Shiite sect of Islam. A rival Islamic group—the Sunnis—runs the Iraqi government, while Shiites dominate the neighboring state of Iran. The two religious branches are frequently at odds.

Streets in Baghdad are often narrow, with crowded and sometimes crumbling buildings lining each side. Wartime damage is also a part of the cityscape, but a plan for urban renewal is under way.

A young vendor carries a tray of bread through a Baghdad bazaar.

in the area. When Iraq became an independent nation in 1932, Baghdad was chosen as its capital, and the new Iraqi government brought the city back to international prominence. Bombing attacks in the 1980s have again altered the face of the city, but Baghdad remains an Iraqi industrial center, processing food, cement, and oil products.

## Secondary Cities

The recent warfare between Iraq and Iran drove many Iraqis from the countryside into the northern cities. Two-thirds of Iraq's people now live in urban areas, which are growing at a fast rate.

Although it lies 75 miles from the Persian Gulf, Basra (population 1.6 million) is Iraq's chief port. The city's southern location at the head of the Shatt al-Arab made it a target for Iranian bombing raids. The war seriously damaged Basra's oil plants, and much of the population left the city. Closed to navigation throughout the 1980s, Basra contains the facilities—including an airport, railways, and several refining complexes—to regain its former commercial position.

The main city of northern Iraq, Mosul is situated on the west bank of the Tigris. Since the 1930s, Mosul has owed its prosperity to the oil fields of the surrounding countryside. Before that time, cotton weaving was the city's chief source of income. Centuries ago, Mosul was famous for its fine cotton cloth (called *muslin*), and weaving is still a major activity. The city also trades locally produced wool, animal hides, and nuts.

Most of Mosul's nearly 1.2 million residents are Arab and Kurdish Muslims. Large numbers of Arab Christians also live in the region. As a result, Christian and Muslim holy places stand side by side in the city. Adding to the area's historical variety are the ruins of Nineveh—the ancient capital of the Assyrian Empire—which lie across the Tigris from Mosul.

appeared in the center of the city. Extending outward from the middle of Baghdad are a wide variety of factories and many residential areas.

Although a small settlement existed on the site as long ago as 4000 B.C., Baghdad became famous in A.D. 762. In that year, the leader of the expanding Islamic empire chose the village as his headquarters. Within a few decades, Baghdad was a hub of Islamic learning and culture. The city's three-part walled structure—with a royal enclosure at the center, army quarters beyond, and ordinary dwellings at the outermost edge—remained standing for several hundred years. Trade areas were outside of the walls.

Destroyed by Asian invaders in 1258, Baghdad declined in status and population for many centuries. By the early eighteenth century, only a few thousand people lived

Kirkuk (population 535,000), in northeastern Iraq, is another city built on oil profits. Once a center for agricultural products such as fruits and grains, Kirkuk has become an important petroleum hub. Several oil pipelines begin at Kirkuk and run westward through Syria, Lebanon, and Turkey to ports on the Mediterranean coast. Iraq's largest Kurdish city, Kirkuk is also the end point of a major railway that begins in Baghdad.

## Religious Sites

Iraq contains several sites that have religious significance for the nation's Shiite Muslims. Because they are also meaningful to Iranian Shiites, the cities largely escaped bombings during the 1980s.

At Al-Najaf in southern Iraq is a shrine to Ali—a seventh-century leader who founded the Shiite sect of the Islamic religion. The Sunni sect formed the majority of the Islamic population, but Sunnis and Shiites differed on various religious issues. After Ali was assassinated, his followers began to honor him as a martyr to the Shiite cause.

Originally built 1,000 years ago, Ali's tomb was subsequently sacked by foreign invaders. A new shrine replaced it in the sixteenth century. Each year, pilgrims from Iran, India, Pakistan, and Afghanistan visit Al-Najaf to worship.

Thousands of Shiite Muslims also travel to Karbala on an annual pilgrimage. Located southwest of Baghdad, the city is the burial place of Husayn, a grandson of Muhammad (the founder of the Islamic religion). In A.D. 680, Husayn was killed in a revolt against the Sunnis. As a result, Shiites regard his tomb as a holy place and mark the date of his death with prayers of mourning.

Photo by Reuters/Bettmann Newsphotos

A resident of Basra stands amid the rubble of his home after a bombing raid in 1987. Located about 75 miles from the Persian Gulf, the city was a major target for Iranian attacks throughout the 1980s.

Independent Picture Service

Mosul, in northern Iraq, contains a variety of architectural styles, including a centuries-old Islamic tower.

A weary Muslim (follower of Islam) rests beneath an ornate archway at the shrine of Husayn, a Shiite martyr. Located in Karbala, this mosque faces another holy place dedicated to the leader Abbas, and the two sites draw thousands of the faithful every year.

The land between the Tigris and Euphrates rivers—called Mesopotamia by the Greeks—hosted many ancient civilizations. This map shows some of the most important sites that thrived and declined over a period of several thousand years. Small settlements (indicated in green) formed in about 5000 B.C., giving way to larger city-states (purple) and later to regional administrations (red). (The boundaries reflect the current borders of Iraq.)

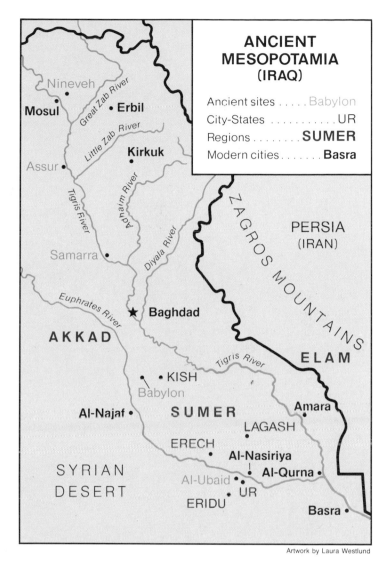

ANCIENT
MESOPOTAMIA
(IRAQ)

Ancient sites . . . . . Babylon
City-States . . . . . . . . . . . UR
Regions . . . . . . . SUMER
Modern cities . . . . . . . Basra

Artwork by Laura Westlund

# 2) History and Government

The most famous events of Iraq's diverse and well-documented history have taken place mainly in the valley between the Tigris and Euphrates rivers. This region was the home of some of the world's most influential cultures. Historians call the area the Fertile Crescent, and conquering Greeks named it Mesopotamia, which means "between the rivers."

In northern Iraq, archaeologists have unearthed the ruins of several Stone-Age communities. These finds suggest that around 6500 B.C. once-nomadic humans ceased to roam and began to construct permanent dwellings. They cultivated crops, tamed wild animals, and lived peacefully with other peoples.

About 5000 B.C., the Ubaidians, a northern people from what is now Iran, moved southward toward fertile parts of the Tigris-Euphrates Valley. They sowed new crops and built mud homes, naming their settlements Eridu, Ur, Lagash, and Kish. The crops and villages thrived and attracted Semitic-speaking peoples who inhabited the Syrian Desert to the west and the Arabian Peninsula to the south. From this early cultural mixture developed Sumer—Iraq's first major civilization.

## The Sumerians

Located in southeastern Iraq, Sumer flourished under a succession of powerful rulers. They expanded the small settlements that already existed. By about 3500 B.C., the region's urban areas—called city-states —contained thousands of people.

A small clay tablet shows the cuneiform ("wedge-shaped") writing that the Sumerians invented. Scribes etched picture-symbols using a tool called a stylus, which left an imprint shaped like a wedge.

| Symbol in use about 3100 B.C. | Symbol in use about 2500 B.C. | Symbol in use about 1800 B.C. | Symbol in use about 600 B.C. | SUMERIAN WORD (translation) |
|---|---|---|---|---|
| | | | | SE (grain) |
| | | | | KUB (mountain) |
| | | | | GUD (ox) |
| | | | | KU(A) (fish) |

Artwork by Laura Westlund

This chart shows the evolution of some common words from a purely illustrated form *(far left)* to a picture-symbol *(middle columns)*. Eventually, scribes related cuneiform characters to sounds *(far right)*. In this way, they could spell any word in the Sumerian language.

Wise farming methods fostered Sumer's wealth. Sumerian engineers built irrigation canals to control the unpredictable waters of the Tigris and Euphrates. This new system of governing the rivers brought water to much of the Lower Plain, allowing orchards, date forests, and grain fields to grow.

The Sumerians were not only good farmers. They also developed powerful weapons and accurate measurements of time and area. Sumerian literature—such as the *Epic of Gilgamesh* and the story of the Great Flood (found later in Jewish and Christian sacred writings)—established Sumer as one of the most advanced cultures in the ancient world. Also of importance were Sumerian religious leaders. Their temples, called *ziggurats,* were impressive pyramids of brick. Sumerian priests advised rulers on many key agricultural, commercial, and political questions.

Sumer's leaders established trade routes to what are now Turkey and Iran. Merchants exchanged locally produced grain and cloth for foreign metals. The heavy trade demanded complex recordkeeping and thus may have encouraged the development of a writing system called *cuneiform,* meaning "wedge-shaped."

Despite its high level of sophistication, Sumer was not unified. Each of its many city-states—including Ur, Erech, Eridu, Kish, and Lagash—was powerful. Bitter struggles for supremacy among the rulers of the city-states were partly responsible for Sumer's decline. In addition, other peoples in the region, many of whom spoke Semitic languages, attacked the small realms.

## Early Conquerors

In about 2300 B.C., under their strong leader Sargon, Semitic-speakers living in Sumer conquered various Sumerian city-states. Sargon established Akkad as his capital, and the Akkadians absorbed many

Sumerian traditions. Other Semitic-speaking groups dislodged the Akkadians. Among the newcomers were the Amorites, a people originally from Syria, who founded their capital at Babylon in the northern part of the Lower Plain.

Eventually called Babylonians, the new conquerors had gained complete control of the Tigris-Euphrates region by about 1800 B.C. Hammurabi, the sixth king of Babylon, used force to mold the rival city-states into a unified realm. A strong war leader, Hammurabi was also a skillful diplomat who respected the culture he had conquered and adopted many of its customs.

Some historians believe that this life-sized bronze head represents Sargon, king of Akkad. A good example of Akkadian art, the piece was deliberately damaged in ancient times.

Photo by Lauros-Giraudon, Louvre Museum

Hammurabi created one of the world's first complete systems of justice, called the Code of Hammurabi. This document attempted to ensure that the strong did not hurt the weak and included strict punishments for offenses. Hammurabi's laws combined the king's ideas with those of earlier legal practices and covered issues that affected property, taxes, labor, and family affairs. The code was the foundation of many other judicial systems in the region.

After Hammurabi died in 1750 B.C., his empire began to crumble. By 1600 B.C., the Hittites—a non-Semitic, Indo-European group that had conquered most of what is now Turkey—had plundered Babylonia, leaving it weak and unprotected. The Kassites, another non-Semitic people, came down from the Zagros Mountains to seize control in about 1570 B.C. They ruled for the next four centuries.

Although archaeologists know little about the Kassite period, it was a prosperous time when all of Babylonia came under one rule. Excavations have unearthed large amounts of diplomatic correspondence, suggesting that Kassite kings were active in the region's affairs.

In the thirteenth and twelfth centuries B.C., the entire area near the eastern Mediterranean—including present-day Turkey, Syria, Jordan, and Iraq—experienced a period of severe upheaval. Floods, famine, civil wars, and invasions were common. In 1150 B.C., invading Elamites from the east removed the Kassite ruler and destroyed the capital. For several centuries, Babylonia grew weak under a succession of rulers who could not unite the population.

**A seven-foot stela, or stone pillar, carries the image of the Babylonian king Hammurabi *(left)* honoring the god of justice. Hammurabi's laws, which state the punishments for various crimes, are written beneath the carving in 49 vertical columns.**

This artwork of an Assyrian soldier dates from the late eighth century B.C. The Assyrian Empire developed in northern Iraq and relied on strong warriors to enforce its rule.

## Foreign Invaders

The Assyrians—an ancient, warlike people who lived in Assur north of the Tigris-Euphrates Plain—began to expand their empire in the ninth century B.C. By the mid-eighth century B.C., their leader Tiglath-pileser III had named himself king of Babylonia. His successors made Nineveh (located near modern Mosul) the capital of Assyria.

To control their vast empire, the Assyrians used harsh methods, which caused many rebellions among conquered peoples. By the early 600s B.C., revolts by the Chaldeans—a local people who inhabited the marshlands of southern Sumer—had toppled the Assyrians. The rebels destroyed several Assyrian cities, including Nineveh and Calah.

Perhaps the most famous Chaldean king was Nebuchadrezzar II, who reigned from 605 to 562 B.C. One of Nebuchadrezzar's main goals was to rebuild Babylon. He ordered magnificent palaces and tall temples to be constructed within the city's strong wall. Above the royal palace were the king's beautiful gardens—called the Hanging Gardens of Babylon. Rising 300 feet above another section of the city was a tower dedicated to the god Marduk (sometimes called the Tower of Babel).

### PERSIAN AND GREEK INFLUENCE

Despite the ambitions of Nebuchadrezzar II, Babylonia remained an unstable state. Clashes between the monarchy and religious leaders weakened the realm. By 539 B.C., the expansion plans of the Achaemenids from neighboring Persia (modern Iran) were aimed at Babylonia. Cyrus, the first of Persia's Achaemenid rulers, took

Although only partly visible, a mosaic from the fourth century B.C. illustrates Alexander the Great in battle. Conflicts between Alexander and Darius III, the last king of the Achaemenid family, signaled the end of Persian rule. After defeating Darius, Alexander led his troops into Babylonia in 331 B.C. and died there in 323 B.C.

Issued in the year of Alexander's death, this silver tetradrachm coin shows the head of Hercules on the front *(top)* and the Greek god Zeus on the back. Around the edge of the coin are the words "Alexander the king" in Greek.

the city, and his heirs harshly governed the region. The Babylonians frequently rebelled, but the area remained in Persian hands until 331 B.C. In that year, the young Greek general Alexander the Great and his troops marched into Babylonia. The Babylonians welcomed the Greeks as liberators from Persian control.

Alexander had bold plans for his empire, which was to be centered in Babylon, but he died in 323 B.C., before much work could be done. Imperial power came into the hands of Alexander's generals. Seleucus, head of Alexander's Greek cavalry, took over Mesopotamia, as the Greeks called the Tigris-Euphrates Valley. He founded the Seleucid dynasty (family of rulers), which eventually ruled a large portion of the Middle East.

Under the Greeks, the city of Babylon lost some of its prominence, but it remained on major trade routes and exchanged a variety of goods with other realms. In addition, Greek scholars introduced ancient Sumerian texts on as-

The profile *(left)* of the Parthian king Mithradates II appears on a silver coin minted during his reign (123–88 B.C.). The back of the coin shows the king on his throne, with "Mithradates the king" around the rim. The Parthians had gained control of Mesopotamia by 126 B.C.

tronomy and mathematics to a growing Greek scientific community.

Seleucid control lasted for about two centuries. By 126 B.C., the Parthians—a nomadic people from central Asia—had captured Mesopotamia. Within a few centuries, another Persian conqueror—Ardashir I of the Sasanian dynasty—dislodged the Parthians. By A.D. 227, Sasanian occupation was complete. During the 400 years

The arch of Ctesiphon *(right)* is one of the highest unsupported arches in the world. Built in the sixth century A.D. by the Sasanian king Khosrow I, the structure is part of his magnificent banqueting hall. The ruins of the ruler's palace lie south of Baghdad.

of Sasanian control, invaders from Italy and Afghanistan frequently harassed the Persians. Busy fending off attacks, the Sasanians did little to develop Mesopotamia. As a result, the irrigation works broke down, and the lush land became infertile.

## Arrival of the Arabs

The Arab conquest of the Mesopotamian city of Kadisiya in A.D. 637 caused the downfall of the Sasanians. A collection of rival clans, the Arabs had become unified under the banner of Islam. The prophet Muhammad founded this one-god religion in what is now Saudi Arabia in the early seventh century A.D. Islam required its followers to expand Islamic territory and to convert non-Islamic peoples.

Muhammad died in 632, and his successors carried the *jihad* (a holy war to spread Islam) to Mesopotamia. Soon after capturing Kadisiya, Umar I—the caliph, or Islamic religious and political leader— founded two cities in Mesopotamia. Al-Kufa became the capital, and Basra was the chief port.

Early in the history of the caliphate (realm of a caliph), an important religious split occurred. The disagreement concerned the method of choosing the next caliph. Arabs who favored an elected leader came to be called Sunni Muslims. Other Arabs— known as Shiite Muslims—supported only descendants of Ali as caliphs. Rivals had

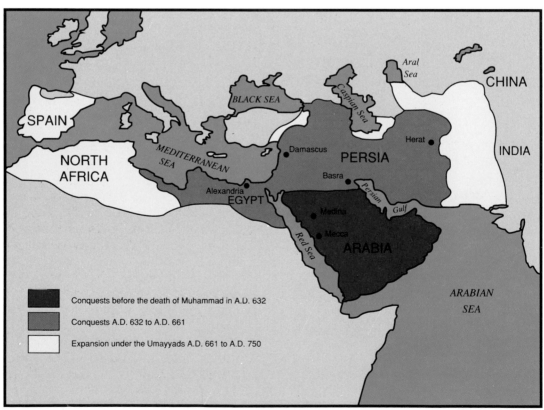

Artwork by Mindy A. Rabin

Armies made up of Muslims from Arabia invaded Mesopotamia in A.D. 633, conquering Ctesiphon in 636 and Kadisiya a year later. The leaders, or caliphs, of the Sunni Umayyad dynasty (family of rulers) established Basra and Al-Kufa as major cities.

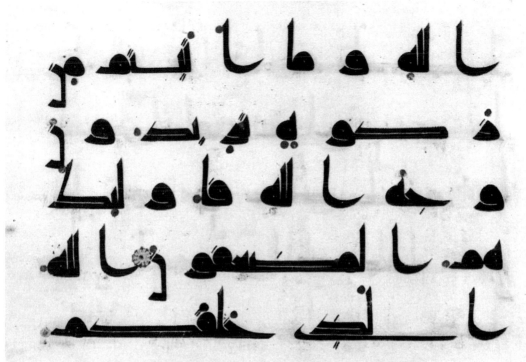

Al-Kufa became a center of Islamic learning, where verses from the Koran—Islam's book of sacred writings—were recorded in a flowing Arabic script called Kufic.

killed Ali, who was the son-in-law of Muhammad, in 661.

### THE ABBASID DYNASTY

By about 665, the more powerful Sunnis controlled the caliphate under the Umayyad dynasty. They established their central city at Damascus (now in Syria). Internal struggles and Shiite rebellions brought down the Umayyad clan, and rival Sunnis of the Abbasid dynasty replaced the Umayyads in 750. The second Abbasid caliph, Abu Jafar al-Mansur, founded the city of Baghdad in 762, making it the capital of his caliphate.

This change in Islamic focus brought great cultural and commercial rewards to Mesopotamia. The round city of Baghdad —so-called because its curved walls enclosed its citizens in wider and wider rings—grew in population and importance. Mathematicians invented Arabic numerals and a decimal system. Engineers repaired the irrigation system. The talented doctor Ibn Sina (called Avicenna in the West) wrote a standard medical text that came to be used throughout Europe and Asia.

The Abbasid caliphate sent ambassadors to many lands. Delegates to China and India returned bearing gifts as tokens of Asian goodwill. The dynasty conducted trade on an enormous scale, and Baghdad became an open market for a wide variety of goods.

These achievements generally occurred in the 800s, when the Abbasid dynasty was at its height and when the empire was at its largest extent. Between the tenth and twelfth centuries, however, the dynasty's control of its vast holdings weakened. Other Islamic groups absorbed pieces of the empire. Within Mesopotamia, caliphs became unifying political symbols but had little real authority.

Surrounded by his students, Ibn Sina (also called Avicenna)—a famous doctor of the Abbasid period—delivers a lecture. Physicians in Europe and Asia used his textbook entitled *Canon of Medicine* for centuries.

Photo by Bettmann Archive

For a short time in the ninth century, the Abbasid court moved to Samarra, where a large kiln (oven for firing pottery) operated. Archaeologists have unearthed gold-and-white plates from the site. The dishes feature animals and people in circular designs.

Courtesy of Freer Gallery of Art, Smithsonian Institution, Washington, D.C.

Independent Picture Service

The ruins at Samarra include an unusual minaret (tower) whose design is based on the ancient *ziggurat,* or temple, used by the Sumerians. Constructed in the mid-ninth century, the minaret has spiral ramps that encircle the column five times, ending at a small room at the top. Historians believe that the tower was part of the largest mosque ever built.

Mamluks—former slaves who had been drafted as Islamic warriors—governed the region in the tenth century. A Shiite military faction held power in the eleventh century, and Seljuk Turks, who belonged to the Sunni sect, ruled in the twelfth century. These various governments—despite being accepted by Abbasid figureheads— suffered from internal rivalries and frequent invasions. Mesopotamia's instability made it easy prey for a new force in world conquest—the Mongols.

## Mongol and Ottoman Control

Originating in central Asia, the warlike Mongols swept through most of the ancient world, laying waste to dozens of historic cities. Under their leader, or khan, Hulegu, the Mongols seized Baghdad in 1258. Hulegu Khan killed the last Abbasid

Photo by Bibliothèque National, Paris

In 1258 the last caliph of Baghdad prepared to surrender his city to the Mongol conqueror Hulegu Khan. The victors executed the caliph and destroyed the city, which for centuries had been an important center of Islamic learning and culture.

caliph. The Mongols smashed the canals that irrigated the Tigris-Euphrates Valley, massacred scholars and writers, and destroyed centuries of Islamic learning and culture. Baghdad lay in ruins, and Mesopotamia became a neglected province of a vast foreign empire. The area remained economically depressed and culturally poor for several centuries.

The Mongols did little to unify their realm, and it eventually split into smaller sections ruled by local leaders. In Mesopotamia, the Jalayirid dynasty held power throughout the 1300s. In 1401, however,

Courtesy of Cultural and Tourism Office of the Turkish Embassy

This sixteenth-century miniature—a small painting of great detail—shows Hulegu Khan surrounded by his soldiers and advisers.

The Ottoman ruler Suleyman I (called the Magnificent) seized Baghdad in 1535, making the city and the former Mongol realm part of the Ottoman Empire. Here, Suleyman *(top center)* rides among his famed troops.

another Mongol force sacked Baghdad, killed most of its inhabitants, and then left the area.

Throughout the 1400s, nomadic and settled peoples competed for control of Mesopotamia. In 1509 Persian troops of the Shiite Safavid dynasty invaded Mesopotamia. They continued to harass the region until Sunnis from the Ottoman Empire (centered in present-day Turkey) expelled them. In 1535 the Ottoman sultan (emperor) Suleyman the Magnificent conquered Baghdad, and Mesopotamia began its 380-year history as part of the Ottoman Empire.

During the period of Ottoman control, Mesopotamia was divided into three provinces—Basra, Baghdad, and Mosul. Each had its own regional problems—such as conflicts between Shiite and Sunni factions,

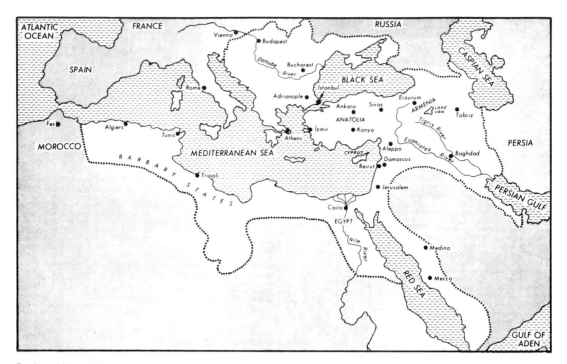

By the middle of the seventeenth century, the vast Ottoman Empire included sections of the Middle East, North Africa, and Eastern Europe. (Map taken from *The Area Handbook for the Republic of Turkey*, 1973.)

between Kurdish and Arab populations, and between Arab and Christian groups. In addition, the Safavids continued to claim Mesopotamian land.

Between the sixteenth and eighteenth centuries, Mesopotamia slowly declined. Occasionally, a talented Ottoman governor would attempt to restore the provinces. More frequently, corrupt administrators, famine, and foreign invasions devastated the region. Yet the area's location and promise of wealth eventually attracted a new group of foreigners—the Europeans.

## European Influence

European nations had traded with Mesopotamia for centuries, but frequent Western contacts did not occur until the early 1800s. The two main powers that became interested in Mesopotamia were Germany and Great Britain. Each country was trying to counterbalance the other's colonial

influence in the region. European innovations soon began to appear in Mesopotamia. Britain sent steamboats up the rivers in 1836, and the Germans laid telegraph lines in 1861. The Germans also proposed a railway to connect the Ottoman city of Konya to Baghdad and later to link Baghdad to Basra.

The British wanted to prevent German expansion in areas that would limit their own colonial trade. As a result, the British made alliances with other European powers and with local Islamic leaders to curb Germany's influence. In addition, Britain had become aware of the untapped oil wealth of the Middle East and sought to gain valuable oil rights throughout the region. The foreign interferences of Britain and Germany sparked several Arab nationalist movements in the early 1900s. In various ways, these organizations sought greater self-rule for Arab populations throughout the Middle East.

World War I broke out in 1914, just when the Arab independence movements were gaining momentum. The global conflict pitted Germany, Austria, and the Ottoman Empire against Britain and France. Arab leaders in many parts of the Arab world—including the Hashemite family of Hussein ibn Ali—promised to aid Britain by revolting against the Ottoman Turks. Arab cooperation came about when Britain agreed to recognize Arab independence after the war. Hussein and his sons, notably Prince Faisal, envisioned a single independent Arab kingdom. They sent their best desert warriors to fight alongside the British against the Ottomans.

British troops occupied Basra in 1915, and they had control of Baghdad by 1917. A year later, the British forces headed north, taking Mosul in October 1918. By the end of the war, the British held all of Mesopotamia.

## The Mandate Period

At the postwar peace conferences, Arab leaders expected to work out the details of Arab independence. But in 1920 the international League of Nations assigned pieces of the Ottoman Empire to the victors, putting Mesopotamia under a British administration. This arrangement, called a mandate, meant that Britain would establish responsible Arab government in the territory according to a league-approved timetable. To many Mesopotamians, being a mandated territory was the same as being a colony.

The failure of the British to fulfill their promises of independence encouraged Arab nationalism. Anti-British secret societies formed in Mesopotamia, and riots broke out in 1920. The strongest protests, which were centered in Mosul, gained support and moved southward. With great difficulty, the British suppressed the rebellion, which Iraqis now call the Great Iraqi Revolution.

Because of the unrest, Britain chose to limit its commitment to the mandated territory in 1921. Aided by British advisers, the Arabs established a constitutional monarchy, called the Kingdom of Iraq. (*Iraq* comes from an Arabic word meaning "the cliffs.") A king and his descendants would head the state. The government would consist of a council of ministers, or cabinet, chosen from a representative assembly. The British asked Prince Faisal to be Iraq's first king, and a nationwide vote confirmed the choice. It was clear, however, that King Faisal I—who was not a native Iraqi—owed his throne to the British.

Although more self-governing, Iraq was still a British mandate. In 1922 Britain signed a treaty with Iraq that promised complete independence to the new kingdom within 10 years. The arrangement

Photo by Bettmann Archives

Prince Faisal was a leader in the Arab revolt against Ottoman rule in World War I (1914–1918). During the postwar peace conferences, Western powers—mainly Britain and France—carved up former Ottoman territories. In 1921 the Europeans made Faisal king of Iraq but allowed the realm only limited self-rule.

While Iraq was under a British administration, oil was discovered near Kirkuk. British firms soon set up drilling rigs in the barren landscape of the north.

A coin from the reign of Faisal's son, Ghazi I, carries Arabic words that read "Ghazi I, King of Iraq" *(front)* and "Kingdom of Iraq" *(back)*. Minted in 1938, the piece had a value of 50 *fils,* or less than one *dinar* – the national monetary unit.

displeased some of Iraq's ethnic and religious groups—notably the Kurds of the north and the Shiite Arabs of the Euphrates River Valley. These groups were not well represented in the nation's newly formed assembly. Both factions wanted to separate their lands from those of Iraq. Because of the resulting violence and unrest, Britain decided to maintain a military force in the country.

The 10-year mandate period brought many improvements to Iraq. With British help, the new nation built schools and medical clinics and updated railways and port facilities. Repaired irrigation works controlled the flow of the Tigris and Euphrates rivers, and new industries received government funding. The Iraqis improved the long-used Ottoman tax system and revised the national legal code.

The most important change came with the discovery of huge oil fields near Kirkuk in 1927. The Iraqis granted oil rights to the Iraq Petroleum Company—a British-dominated, multinational firm. The company began to explore the region, and it built pipelines that stretched westward to ports on the Mediterranean Sea.

## Independence and World War II

In accordance with the 1922 treaty, Iraq became formally independent in 1932, but the nation still had strong ties to Great Britain. To protect its growing oil interests in the Middle East, Britain kept up its military presence in Iraq.

Within a year of Iraq's independence, King Faisal I died. His death unleashed conflicts that had been brewing for several years. The Shiites still feared the domination of the Sunnis, who occupied most administrative and political posts. The Kurds—who strongly favored separation from the rest of Iraq—asserted their claim to their own nation, called Kurdistan. The

Assyrians—a Christian, pro-British group in northeastern Iraq—voiced a similar demand. The Assyrians were also concerned about postindependence actions against them by Islamic and anti-British factions in the country.

Faisal's son and successor, Ghazi, lacked his father's unifying prestige and experience. He was unable to balance conflicting religious and ethnic demands. In addition, the army entered the political arena and used its power to dismiss several cabinets. Army officers caused many of the cabinet changes that occurred in the 1930s and 1940s.

Amid this instability, King Ghazi died in an automobile accident in 1939. Faisal's three-year-old grandson inherited the throne as Faisal II. The young king's cousin, Prince Abd al-Ilah, ruled for him as regent. Within months of Ghazi's death, World War II (1939–1945) broke out. The regent and the prime minister, Nuri al-Said, favored a pro-British stance during the global conflict. But widespread anti-British feelings existed in the nation. Rashid Ali al-Kaylani—who replaced Nuri as prime minister in a cabinet shuffle in 1941—shared these sentiments.

Rashid Ali sought close ties with Nazi Germany to release Iraq from British domination. When the British asked permission to land some soldiers in Iraq in April 1941, the Iraqi government did not fully cooperate. In response, the British sent troops to Basra, where they clashed with the Iraqi army. By the end of May, the British had the upper hand, and the prime minister fled to Egypt. A pro-British government was assembled, and Iraq became a wartime base for British and U.S. forces stationed in the Middle East.

### POSTWAR EVENTS

In 1945, the year the war ended, Iraq became a founding member of two important organizations. The Arab League was formed in March to strengthen ties between Arab countries in the Middle East. In December Iraq also joined the United Nations (UN).

In 1947 the UN split nearby Palestine into an Arab and a Jewish state, a move that the Arab League strongly resented. Following the creation of the Jewish State of Israel in 1948, members of the Arab League, including Iraq, sent troops to crush the new nation. Fighting lasted for several months, until the UN arranged a cease-fire. Iraq, however, remained opposed to a Jewish homeland in the Middle East. Most Iraqi Jews—who made up a small portion of the national population—emigrated to Israel.

Oil and oil profits were among the major issues facing Iraq in the 1950s. After the Iraqis granted oil rights to foreigners, the petroleum industry flourished. But most of the money from oil ventures left the country. In the early 1950s, the Iraq Petroleum Company (IPC) negotiated a

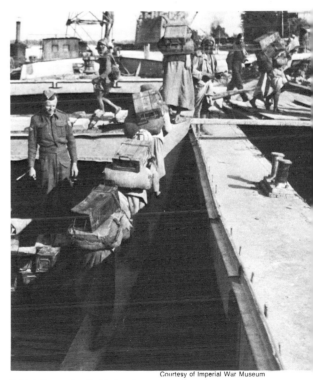

Courtesy of Imperial War Museum

**British forces landed in Iraq in 1941 and set up supply stations for battles during World War II (1939-1945).**

new accord with Iraq. Under this arrangement, the nation obtained 50 percent of the oil profits, much of which were set aside for internal development. In an attempt to gain more bargaining power with foreign-owned oil companies, Iraq became a founding member of the Organization of Petroleum Exporting Countries (OPEC).

## Revolution and Socialism

Although it gained some wealth in the 1950s, Iraq was still a poor nation. A wide gap existed between rich and poor and between pro-Western and pro-Arab activists. The government, which was often run by Nuri al-Said or his handpicked supporters, lobbied for Western aid. Middle- and low-income groups were attracted by the anti-Western, pan-Arab sentiments of neighboring nations, especially Egypt. (Pan-Arabism supports regional unity and political cooperation in the Arab world.)

Internal disagreements grew until 1958, when General Abdul Karim Kassem and Colonel Abd al-Salam Arif led a coup d'état (forceful government takeover). During bloody fighting, Nuri, Prince Abd al-Ilah,

and King Faisal II were killed. Following the coup, which Iraqis celebrate as the 1958 Revolution, Iraq declared itself a republic.

The leaders of the coup formed a new government, with Kassem as its head. Pan-Arabism—particularly the kind of broad-based Arab unity supported in Egypt—was popular in Iraq, but Kassem was against the movement. He repressed pan-Arab and other political activities that disagreed with his views. By the early 1960s, the Kassem regime had lost support. A military coup in 1963 deposed Kassem, who was later killed.

Members of the Syrian-based Baath party organized the overthrow, and one of the party's leaders, Ahmad Hasan al-Bakr, became prime minister. Abd al-Salam Arif, a supporter of Pan-Arabism, was named president. The new government declared Iraq to be a socialist country. Arif eventually forced al-Bakr from office, beginning a round of coups and countercoups that lasted through the 1960s.

In 1968 al-Bakr staged a final overthrow. Members of a remolded Baath party—which was now more socialist and less tied

Independent Picture Service

In the 1960s, citizens of Baghdad passed beneath a monument that commemorates the overthrow of the monarchy and the establishment of the Republic of Iraq in 1958.

Iraq invaded Iran in September 1980. Since then, thousands of civilians and soldiers on both sides have died or been wounded. The United Nations arranged a cease-fire in 1988, but each country still holds many prisoners of war. These Iraqis wait to be released from a camp in southwestern Iran.

to the Syrian Baath party—assumed complete control of the government. The Iraqi Baath party's goal was to create a strong state that could influence other nations in the Middle East. Socialist principles—including shared ownership of farms and industries and the elimination of social inequalities—guided the new government. Chief among al-Bakr's colleagues was Saddam Hussein, who became a key participant in the Revolutionary Command Council (RCC) that ran the country.

Iraq's oil industry underwent changes in the 1970s. In 1972 Iraq nationalized (switched from private ownership to state control) the IPC. The government began to operate the Kirkuk fields as part of the Iraqi Company for Oil Operations. IPC members received compensation for the takeover of their facilities. Later nationalizations brought other foreign oil

companies under state ownership. The government set up the Iraqi National Oil Company to manage the country's entire oil industry.

## Recent Events

Throughout the 1970s, the issue of Kurdistan—the self-governing nation proposed by the region's Kurds—sharply divided Iraq. In 1970 the RCC agreed to grant the Kurds self-rule eventually, and it named Kurdish as one of Iraq's official languages. Few real concessions of political power were made, however, and Kurdish resentment grew. In 1974 clashes between Kurdish guerrillas—called the *Pesh Merga,* or "those who face death"—and Iraqi soldiers occurred.

Iran—a traditional enemy of Iraq—sympathized with the Iraqi Kurds and sent them weapons. In 1975, however, Iran signed an agreement with Iraq cutting off aid to the Kurdish rebels. This move disabled the revolt, and by 1976 all Kurdish resistance had ceased. During this period, ill health began to affect al-Bakr's ability to govern. In 1979 al-Bakr resigned in favor of Saddam Hussein, who became president of Iraq.

### IRAN-IRAQ WAR

The 1975 Iran-Iraq agreement did more than stop Iran's support of the Kurds. It also tried to settle a long-standing boundary dispute over the Shatt al-Arab. In 1980, however, Iraq demanded a revision of the agreement, which Iran rejected. Iraqi forces invaded Iran in September of that year.

The conflict highlighted the centuries-old differences between Sunni and Shiite Muslims. Although Sunnis dominate Iraq's power structure, 55 percent of the nation's population are Shiites. Iran, a Shiite Islamic state, hoped that a call for Islamic unity would topple the nonreligious regime of Iraq's President Hussein. In addition, the Pesh Merga allied itself with Iran against Iraq in the war.

In the 1980s, thousands of Iranian and Iraqi civilians and soldiers were wounded, killed, or captured. Iraq spent about $35 billion of its own money on the war and amassed a foreign debt of over $40 billion. In the course of the fighting, Basra suffered heavy casualties, and its port facilities were shut down. Iraq in turn bombed Iran's oil facilities on the Persian Gulf. As a result of the destruction, the oil production of Iraq and Iran fell. The war limited the ability of both nations and of neutral Arab states to ship oil through the Persian Gulf.

Most Arab countries in the region did not support Iran's fight and sent funds to Iraq. Hussein's warlike stance remained popular among most Iraqis. Iranians, on the other hand, strongly supported their own government in the conflict. Clashes

Photo © Christina Dameyer/S. F. Photo Network

Iraqis continue to support President Saddam Hussein, who came to power in 1979. Here, a young girl in Mosul raises a large photo of the chief executive amid a cheering crowd.

and counter-offensives occurred year after year.

Both sides also engaged in a war of words, in which Iran promoted itself as an ideal Islamic state and branded Iraq as an illegal, unreligious regime. Iraq countered these claims by appealing to national rather than religious loyalties. Although the Hussein government suppressed anti-Iraqi Shiite factions within the country, the regime also promised not to interfere with nonpolitical Shiite activities. In this way, Hussein gained the support of the Shiite Arabs in Iraq.

By the mid-1980s, the war had reached a stalemate, with neither side gaining new ground. The Arab League called for Iran and Iraq to agree to a UN-sponsored cease-fire. Iraq accepted the cease-fire in 1987, and Iran consented to it a year later. The agreement arranged for the future exchange of prisoners and for the withdrawal of troops.

Soon after the cease-fire, the Iraqi army attacked Kurdish guerrillas who had sided with Iran. Entire Kurdish villages were destroyed, and international groups charged Iraq with using outlawed poison gas to kill Kurdish civilians. Although substantial evidence exists, Iraq has denied the charges.

The 1988 cease-fire also provided Iraq with time to examine the damage to its oil industry. In addition, the fragile peace has given Iraq the opportunity to address some internal concerns regarding health, education, housing, and jobs. If the cease-fire holds, Iraq may be able to enter a new era of growth in the 1990s.

## Government

Iraq has an informal constitution, and most legislative and executive powers are in the hands of the nine-member RCC, which is dominated by army officers. The chairman of the council is also president of the republic, prime minister, and commander of the armed forces. In June 1980, Iraqis elected a 250-member national assembly, but it has limited legislative power.

A court of cassation (appeal)—Iraq's highest civil court—hears cases in Baghdad. The court consists of at least nine permanent members and six appointed members. In addition, there are courts of first instance and sharia courts. The latter group deals with religious matters and makes decisions based on traditional Islamic law.

For local administrative purposes, Iraq is organized into 18 governorates, which are subdivided into smaller political districts. An appointed governor, who has broad local powers, administers each governorate. Three of the governorates, each of which contains a Kurdish majority, have limited self-rule.

Artwork by Laura Westlund

Iraq's flag, which was adopted after a government takeover in 1963, features colors that have associations throughout the Arab world. Red stands for courage, and white represents generosity. Black is a reminder of the conquests of Islam, and green is the religion's traditional color.

In Al-Nasiriya, a town in southern Iraq, a young boy grins at his baby brother. About 45 percent of the nation's population is under the age of 15.

# 3) The People

Iraq's population of 18.1 million people includes several ethnic groups. Arabs make up about 75 percent of the total, and Kurds —the largest non-Arab group—compose about 20 percent. Small numbers of Turkomans, Assyrians, Armenians, and Iranians also live in Iraq.

The country's landscape affects the distribution of its people. Villages are spread evenly throughout the river valleys, where many Iraqis farm the land. Nomadic herders still roam the deserts and plains in search of food for their camels, sheep, and goats. Many Iraqis moved to urban areas during the Iran-Iraq war, and their numbers have put pressure on housing, jobs, and basic services in most cities.

Although male Iraqis share the traditional Islamic view of women as mothers and homemakers, the recent war brought many females into the work force. Women now hold some important administrative and political positions. Most urban Iraqi women do not wear the full-length covering that is commonly seen in Islamic countries.

## Ethnic Groups

Throughout its long history, Iraq has absorbed many related groups. These peoples have left their ethnic imprints on Iraq's population, creating a rich mixture of Arabs.

Two minority groups—the Madan and the Bedouin—stand out among Iraq's Arabs. The Madan, who are also called Marsh Arabs, inhabit the swamplands near the mouth of the Shatt al-Arab. Living in tall reed homes that have arched roofs, most male Marsh Arabs are fishermen. Several families make up each Madan village, and one dwelling is set aside for guests. Long, open boats take people from house to house and from village to village.

Far from the water-based homes of the Madan are the lands of the Bedouin. These desert wanderers travel through the hot zones of Iraq, Saudi Arabia, Kuwait, and Jordan on a seasonal search for water and grass for their livestock. Iraq and Saudi Arabia each gave up a piece of their desert territory to form a neutral zone to ease the movements of the Bedouin between the two countries. In recent years, however, many Bedouin have adopted more settled ways of life.

Traditionally, the Bedouin live in large woven tents. Each tent represents a family, and a group of families makes up a clan. The Bedouin have a strong sense of family and clan loyalty, and they are also famous for their courage and hospitality.

Iraq's largest non-Arab group is the Kurds. These semi-nomads often farm or herd livestock to make a living. Although Kurds follow the Sunni sect of the Islamic religion, they have long fought against

Women have become an important part of the Iraqi work force. Here, modern clothing distinguishes these computer users at the National Office of Tourism.

Photo © Christina Dameyer/S. F. Photo Network

Photo by EDR Media

A Bedouin folds the wool tent that shelters the family during its stays in the desert. Although of different clans, the Bedouin of Iraq, Syria, Saudi Arabia, Kuwait, and Jordan have similar lifestyles.

other Muslims to establish their own nation. Iraq's Kurds share ethnic ties with Kurds of Turkey, Iran, Syria, and the Soviet Union. These ties and a strong sense of cultural identity have fueled the group's 70-year struggle for self-rule.

Smaller minorities are scattered throughout Iraq. Assyrians live in the Zagros

Photo © Christina Dameyer/S. F. Photo Network

These Kurds wear traditional ethnic clothing in Erbil, a Kurdish city in northeastern Iraq. Historians believe that Erbil may be one of the oldest continuously inhabited settlements in the world.

Photo © Christina Dameyer/S. F. Photo Network

En route to Tall Afar—a town near Mosul—an Iraqi Turkoman stops to display his prayerbook.

Mountains and near Mosul. Armenians, whose ancestors fled Ottoman attempts to destroy them during World War I, form a strong trading community in Baghdad.

Although the Assyrians and the Armenians belong to Christian sects, both groups have been accepted into Iraqi society.

Turkomans live in villages between Kirkuk and Mosul. Originally from Ottoman Turkey, Iraq's Turkomans also share ethnic ties with peoples in the Soviet Union. Because of the war, few people with Iranian backgrounds have remained in Iraq. Most of Iraq's Iranian population cluster near the holy cities of Karbala, Al-Najaf, and Samarra.

## Language and Literature

The majority of Iraqis speak Arabic, one of the nation's official languages and the main tongue of the Arab world. Three styles of Arabic exist in Iraq. The Koran, the book of Islamic sacred writings, is written in classical Arabic. Almost any Arabic-speaker can understand modern standard Arabic, a later literary language. Within Iraq, a separate dialect called Iraqi Arabic is used in daily speech.

The Assyrians speak Syriac, a Semitic tongue that is related to Arabic. The Kurds use either of two Kurdish dialects that have their roots in the Indo-Iranian family of languages. The Turkomans employ a southern Turkic speech, which is also spoken in parts of the Soviet Union.

Read from right to left, Arabic letters are written in different styles. Thickly drawn characters (top row) are for everyday use, while a more flowing form (middle row) is used for special occasions. The most ornate lettering (bottom row) appears primarily in headlines and titles. Although many dialects of spoken Arabic exist, the written language is the same throughout the Arab world.

المملكة العربية السعودية

المملكة العربية السعودية

المملكة العربية السعودية

Independent Picture Service

A collection of Arab folktales, *The Thousand and One Nights* was probably put together between A.D. 1000 and 1500. The underlying narration involves Scheherazade, the new wife of a powerful king who intends to have his bride beheaded. To delay her fate, Scheherazade tells the king a story *(left illustration)*, leaving the conclusion of the tale until the next day. For 1,001 nights, Scheherazade entertains her husband with characters such as Ali Baba *(right illustration)* and Aladdin. After hearing 1,001 tales, the king decides to spare Scheherazade and to keep her as his wife.

Early Iraqi literature has strongly influenced the writings of other cultures. The Christian Bible and sacred Jewish works share themes and subjects—such as creation, the Garden of Eden, and the Great Flood—with ancient tales from Sumer, Babylonia, and Assyria. Among the most famous early epics (long narrative poems) is the Sumerian *Epic of Gilgamesh.* The story follows Gilgamesh, a king of the city-state of Erech, in his search for eternal life.

The Arab conquest of the seventh century introduced vivid poetry and prose to the region, and these forms are still extremely popular in Iraq. Among the folktales that are most famous to Westerners is *The Thousand and One Nights.* This collection of stories describes the adventures of fictional characters such as Aladdin and Sinbad.

Iraqi poetry and prose are meant to be recited, and skilled readers can draw attentive crowds. Iraqi writers and playwrights also use other literary forms to express themselves, but the oral tradition reaches the largest public audience.

## Religion

Most Iraqis are Muslims, but they are split into two rival sects of the Islamic religion. Fifty-five percent are Arab Shiites, who share their beliefs with non-Arab Shiites in Iran. Sunnis, who compose a majority in most other Arab countries, make up about 40 percent of Iraq's religious population. Both sects accept the teachings of Muhammad as recorded in the Koran.

Sunni Muslims directly approach Allah (the Arabic name for God). This form of the Islamic religion provides no clergy and no religious rites. Shiites depend on imams—holy men who deeply understand and follow the Koran and who have earthly and spiritual power—to be intermediaries between the faithful and Allah. For Sunni Muslims, an imam is one who leads other Muslims in prayer. This difference in the imam's role and authority is one result of the split over Islamic leadership in the seventh century.

No matter what the sect, Islam requires that its believers fulfill certain obligations. Among these duties are daily prayer, fasting during the holy month of Ramadan, and making donations to the poor. In addition, male Muslims must try to visit the holy city of Mecca in Saudi Arabia at least once in their lifetime.

A small percentage of Iraqis are Christians, and most follow sects of the Catholic religion. The Assyrians are members of the Nestorian Church, which was founded in Iran in the fifth century. Armenians make up a smaller proportion of Iraq's Christians, and there are also minority communities of Syrian and Chaldean Catholics.

## Health and Education

The government operates most of Iraq's medical facilities. Because doctors and nurses tend to cluster in Baghdad and

A modern mosque in Baghdad is a relatively new addition to the city's holy places. From the tall minaret, loudspeakers broadcast a chant in Arabic that calls faithful Muslims to prayer five times each day.

A Shiite mullah, or Islamic scholar, reads his Koran in a corner of a mosque in Kadhimain. Koranic schools supplement Iraq's educational system with religious studies.

These Iraqi children in Mosul receive instruction in socialist ideas and military tactics, as well as in more traditional subject matters.

other large cities, a major obstacle to providing good health care nationwide is a lack of trained rural personnel.

In recent years, the government has initiated large-scale vaccination programs that aim to reduce cases of diphtheria, tuberculosis, and measles among children. Although 97 percent of urban residents have access to safe water, the figure drops to 22 percent in rural areas. The lack of safe water accounts for many of the water-carried diseases, such as cholera, that are still common in the Iraqi countryside. Life expectancy in Iraq, which is 66 years, is a little above average for western Asia. For the region, the nation has a fairly high infant mortality rate—69 deaths in every 1,000 live births.

In 1958, when the republic was established, only 20 percent of the population could read and write. By the late 1980s, this figure had risen to about 80 percent. Primary education, which is compulsory and free, provides a six-year course at the end of which students must pass an examination to be admitted to secondary school. Secondary schools have a three-year intermediate course followed by a two-year period of study to prepare for college. Almost one million Iraqi youngsters are enrolled in secondary schools.

An increasing number of girls are attending school at the primary and secondary levels. The government has made the education of women a special goal. As a result, the female literacy rate has risen considerably in recent years.

In the 1920s, the British introduced Western styles of higher education to Iraq. Although university schooling is free, some colleges require several years of government service in exchange for tuition. The government also provides its young citizens with vocational training at more than 40 schools with courses in agriculture, business, and home economics. In addition, Islamic schools—particularly those in Al-Najaf and Karbala—are centers of religious education in Iraq.

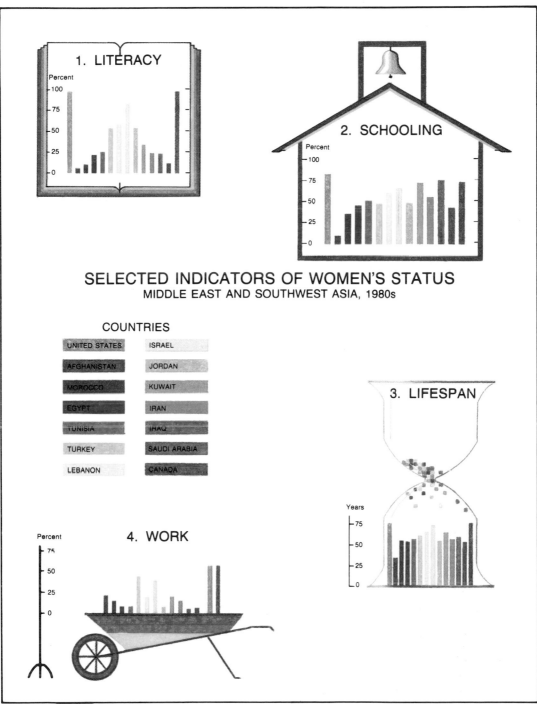

### 1. LITERACY

### 2. SCHOOLING

## SELECTED INDICATORS OF WOMEN'S STATUS
### MIDDLE EAST AND SOUTHWEST ASIA, 1980s

#### COUNTRIES

| | |
|---|---|
| UNITED STATES | ISRAEL |
| AFGHANISTAN | JORDAN |
| MOROCCO | KUWAIT |
| EGYPT | IRAN |
| TUNISIA | IRAQ |
| TURKEY | SAUDI ARABIA |
| LEBANON | CANADA |

### 3. LIFESPAN

### 4. WORK

Artwork by Carol F. Barrett

Depicted in this chart are factors relating to the status of women in the Middle East and southwest Asia. **Graph 1,** labeled Literacy, shows the percentage of adult women who can read and write. **Graph 2** illustrates the proportion of school-aged girls who actually attend elementary and secondary schools. **Graph 3** depicts the life expectancy of female babies at birth. **Graph 4** shows the percentage of women in the income-producing work force. Data taken from *Women in the World: An International Atlas,* 1986 and from *Women . . . A World Survey,* 1985.

## The Arts

The museums of Iraq, especially those in Baghdad, contain examples of ancient artworks from many of Iraq's previous cultures. Carved slabs of stone, delicate jewelry, and fine textiles—as well as the unearthed remains of splendid ancient cities, such as Nineveh and Calah—testify to the nation's long creative tradition.

Because the Koran forbids the use of human figures in Islamic decoration, Arab artistic output in Iraq has focused on geo-metric patterns. The mosaic tile work of mosques and the ornately hand-lettered prayers from the Koran present a stunning variety of styles and shapes. Craftspeople also produce colorful rugs, fine leather goods, and decorative metal items, all of which are sold in urban bazaars.

Music, especially folk music, is a major form of expression in Iraq. Played on tradi-tional instruments—such as the *oud* (an Arabian lute) and the *rebab* (a fiddle)— Iraqi music often accompanies the celebra-

With deft movements, an Iraqi musi-cian plucks a *kanoon* – an ancient in-strument similar to a zither that may have as many as 100 strings.

Independent Picture Service

Photo © Tina Manley/Images

In Baghdad's bazaars, metal crafts-people hammer and decorate their pieces within view of passersby.

Independent Picture Service

Traditional Islamic decoration, which features ornate geometric patterns, adorns the interior of the Martyrs' Mosque in Baghdad.

Independent Picture Service

A modern statue that symbolizes Iraqi women stands in a park in the center of the capital.

tion of important events. Drums and loud chants are also part of Iraqi celebrations. Western classical music exists in urban areas, and Radio Baghdad plays popular tunes. But most Iraqis prefer to hear traditional musical forms and instruments.

## Recreation and Food

Iraqis are enthusiastic sports fans and often watch games of soccer—the country's most popular sport. Television stations carry the matches played between the national league teams, and supporters crowd the stadium in Baghdad.

Basketball, volleyball, weight-lifting, and boxing are also favorite activities. Sports facilities in some areas of the country are limited, but Iraq hopes to develop teams for the Olympics and other international events.

Courtesy of Iraqi Press Office

Members of Iraqi soccer teams play in front of packed audiences in the stadium in Baghdad.

49

A vendor packages thick *samoons*—round, flat pieces of bread—at his stall in Al-Najaf.

Iraqi cuisine is rich and varied, ranging from kebabs (skewered chunks of grilled meat) to *masgouf* (a specialty that uses fish from the Tigris River). Other popular dishes are *quzi* (stuffed roasted lamb) and *kubba* (minced meat, nuts, raisins, and spices). Most meals include *samoons*, flat rounds of wheat bread. Arab coffee—brewed strong, thick, and bitter—is the traditional drink, and tea served in small glasses is also popular. Desserts include fruit and baklava—a pastry made of honey and nuts layered between paper-thin sheets of dough.

Photo © Christina Dameyer/S. F. Photo Network

Photo © Christina Dameyer/S. F. Photo Network

Despite the 1988 cease-fire, Iraqi soldiers are a strong presence in the nation. Here, some off-duty troops enjoy small glasses of tea at an outdoor stand.

The key to Iraq's future prosperity is still found in the nation's oil, most of which is processed at refineries in Kirkuk *(above)*.

# 4)  The Economy

Before warfare broke out between Iraq and Iran in 1980, Iraq had bold plans for economic development. These ideas relied on expected profits from oil sales. Since 1980, however, the government has spent much of its budget on weapons from the Soviet Union, France, and the United States. Iranian bombings of Iraqi pipelines and petroleum facilities decreased Iraq's ability to export oil. The drop in oil income set back the government's plans to expand roads and power plants and to improve the educational and health-care systems.

With the cease-fire of 1988 in place, Iraq may be able to return to its previous economic programs. But the nation begins a new period of growth with a heavy foreign debt and with uncertainty about whether the peace with Iran will last.

## Oil and Mining

The oil industry –the principal source of Iraq's wealth—provides nearly all of the nation's foreign income. Oil production began in 1927, and, by the late 1980s, total crude oil exports amounted to about 700 million barrels per year.

The main oil fields lie in three regions— near Kirkuk, northwest of Mosul, and southwest of Basra. Until recently, the northern deposits of crude oil went by pipeline to Baniyas in Syria, and to Tripoli in Lebanon. Southern oil was piped through Fao, Iraq's port on the Persian

Gulf. Syria—which supported Iran during the war—closed Iraq's access to Mediterranean ports in 1982. Iranian bombings destroyed the Fao connection. Nearly all of Iraq's oil now goes by pipeline through Turkey and Saudi Arabia.

For decades, the Iraq Petroleum Company—which British, U.S., French, and Dutch interests controlled—had a monopoly on Iraqi oil. Between 1972 and 1975, the Iraqi government nationalized most of the country's oil resources and facilities. Since then, the Iraqi National Oil Company has been responsible for exploration, production, transport, and marketing of crude oil and oil products. Wartime losses of export facilities, refining stations, and transnational pipelines caused Iraq's income from oil to vary throughout the 1980s.

The decrease in oil profits limited funds for other mining ventures. As a result, Iraq has made only minor attempts to tap other mineral resources. In 1987, however, a new sulfur plant opened in Mishraq with the help of foreign aid. Iraq may be able substantially to expand its mining industry by exploiting its large sulfur deposits,

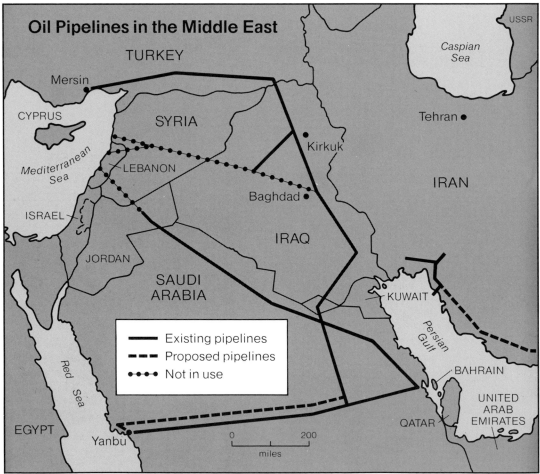

Artwork by Laura Westlund

Throughout the 1980s, Iraq's ability to export its oil has been hampered both by the Iran-Iraq war and by the scarcity of pipelines. Because transport through the Persian Gulf was dangerous, Iraq sent its oil to ports on the Mediterranean and Red seas by way of Turkey and Saudi Arabia.

Oil storage tanks at Fao emit smoke after Iranian planes bombed them in 1987. Half of the port's facilities were damaged or destroyed in the 1980s.

its reserves of brown coal, and its finds of lead, zinc, and other metals.

## Agriculture

Throughout Iraq's history, agricultural setbacks occurred when canals and water pumps failed to control seasonal flooding. Management of the rivers continues to be vital to successful farming in modern times. About 40 percent of Iraq's land can be farmed, but only one-fourth of that amount is actually plowed and planted. Much territory lies unused in a given year to regain fertility, and a substantial portion of the remainder is pasture.

At Amara in southeastern Iraq, a vendor offers some of the nation's huge date harvest for sale. The country produces 95 percent of the world's dates.

Photo by V. Southwell, The Hutchison Library

Controlled irrigation—sometimes provided by ancient waterwheels—is vital to successful farming in Iraq.

In the Upper and Lower plains, irrigation is essential to successful harvests of wheat, barley, corn, grapes, melons, oranges, and rice. In the northeast, where rainfall sup- plies enough water for crops, farmers grow barley, olives, tobacco, and fruits. Dates are by far the most important of Iraq's ex- port crops. The nation is the world's larg-

Photo © Christina Dameyer/S. F. Photo Network

Plentiful fruits and vegetables crowd stalls in a Baghdad market. With careful planning, Iraqi farmers can grow a wide variety of hot-weather crops.

54

Using a horse-drawn plow, a young Iraqi prepares his field for planting.

Photo by EDR Media

est supplier of dates, which flourish along the country's canals and rivers.

Although sheep dominate Iraq's domesticated herds, other livestock—such as cattle, horses, water buffalo, goats, and camels—are also raised. Most herding takes place in the northeast, and modern dairy and poultry farms have been introduced.

In areas of the country where irrigation is not available, many people raise livestock.

Photo by EDR Media

## Industry and Trade

The industrial sector plays a relatively small role in Iraq's economy. Roughly 10 percent of the population have jobs in manufacturing. In addition to refineries that process petroleum and other oil-based goods, Iraq has factories that make textiles, cement, and paper products. Much of the industrial work involves processing agricultural items, such as oil from vegetable seeds, flour from cereal grains, and leather from animal hides.

Iraq's cities, especially the capital, contain nearly all of the nation's manufacturing plants. In recent years, the Soviet Union has helped Iraq to build many new factories, including an asphalt plant, a steel mill, and an electrical equipment factory.

Because Iraq does not make very many industrial products, it must import most manufactured goods. The main imports are electrical machines, farming equipment, vehicles, and chemical products. The nation also buys foodstuffs and weapons from foreign countries. Iraq's chief suppliers are Japan, West Germany, France, the Soviet Union, and the United States.

Crude oil makes up more than 90 percent of Iraq's exports, and the nation sends petroleum to markets in France, Brazil, Italy, West Germany, and Japan. Other exports include cement, dates, raw wool, and hides.

Photo by EDR Media

**Much of Iraq's manufacturing is done by hand. Here, a worker carefully finishes another brick.**

Courtesy of Iraqi Press Office

A team of laborers transfers thread from larger to smaller spools. The textile industry is one of the most mechanized sectors of the nation's economy.

Photo by EDR Media

Pieces of heavy machinery, such as this cargo-laden truck, are among Iraq's major imports.

Iraq's dwindling hardwood forests lie mostly in the northeast, but southern areas contain large groves of date palms.

A fisherman mends his net by hand alongside the Shatt al-Arab.

## Forestry and Fishing

Centuries of careless logging and land clearing have largely destroyed Iraq's forests. Kurdish areas of the northeast still contain valuable stands of oak, maple, pistachio, hawthorn, and juniper trees. Much of the remaining woodlands provide fuel and building materials.

Iraq's small fishing industry focuses on the country's river system and on several lakes. Most of the fish volume, therefore, consists of freshwater species, including carp, barbel, and dace. Large catches come from the Tigris River, and the Marsh Arabs live off their daily hauls of fish from southern waters. Since the war, the Persian Gulf has not been an important source of fish. In 1985 Iraq opened its first fish hatchery. This facility, located in Baghdad, will reduce the nation's dependence on river and canal species.

The Madan are skilled fishermen and take good care of their boats. To seal his vessel, a boatman applies hot tar to the hull *(above)*. Marsh Arabs fish the waters of the Shatt al-Arab, bringing back netfuls of local species for their daily food *(left)*.

## Energy and Transportation

Because of its vast oil reserves, most of Iraq's energy comes from oil-powered plants. Hydropower stations, which have been built along the Tigris River and its tributaries, also generate electricity. The best sites for dams, however, are located on parts of the Tigris that lie in other countries. In 1986 three dams—including a huge, Soviet-built structure at Kadisiya —went into operation on the Euphrates River.

Railways and highways link all of Iraq's major cities. The government owns and operates the state railway, which has about 1,400 miles of track. Rail connections also take passengers to Syria, Turkey, and Europe. Over 6,000 miles of paved roads, including an all-weather highway, link Iraq to neighboring countries. About 250,000 vehicles for passengers and freight use the roads between major Iraqi cities. In rural areas, camels, donkeys, and horses provide transportation.

The Iraqi government owns the national airline—Iraqi Airways—which flies to Europe and to other parts of Asia. The airports at Baghdad and Basra receive international air traffic. Although Basra is still Iraq's main port for oceangoing vessels, the facilities at Umm Qasr handle an increasing volume of shipping. River steamers can navigate the Tigris River between Basra and Baghdad.

Independent Picture Service

Located near Baghdad, this dam harnesses the power of the Tigris River to provide electricity to central Iraq.

A modern diesel train runs on a line that goes from Baghdad to Basra. Much of Iraq's railway system is outdated, overloaded, and slow, but improvements are gradually easing the difficulties of long-distance travel.

Among desert Arabs, horses and camels are the most common forms of transport.

Marsh Arabs use their boats to carry goods, as well as to fish. Here, oarsmen paddle their reed-filled vessels to Al-Qurna on the Shatt al-Arab.

## The Future

Since late 1988, Iraq has cautiously turned some of its attention to internal affairs. The cease-fire with Iran has given the Hussein government a chance to assess the nation's foreign debt and to decide where to direct the country's energies. Oil will remain the economic mainstay, and some funds will likely be set aside to restore damaged production and refining facilities.

The Hussein government continues to be popular, but how it handles long-standing Kurdish demands—whether with force or with negotiation—will help to determine its ultimate success. The peace with Iran, though fragile, offers Iraq time to rebuild itself. In a new era of growth, the nation's citizens may yet receive some of the social and economic benefits that the government has promised.

Many people get around on foot, especially when flooding blocks auto traffic in the rainy season and when dust hampers travel in dry periods.

Despite the issues that divide Iraq and Iran, Iraq's Shiite holy places – such as the mosques at Karbala *(above)* – are open to the nation's Shiite Muslims. During the war, Iranian Shiites tried to enlist the support of Iraqi Shiites, but most of them chose to stay out of the conflict.

Carrying a photograph of President Hussein, this young Iraqi shows pride in being a vanguard, or military cadet. His clothes are printed with a map of the Arab world, of which Iraq is an important part.

# Index